A Collection of Mysterious Myths & Legends

Jo Ann Atcheson Gray

Contents

A Collection of Mysterious Myths & Legends

⸺◦✦◦⸺

A Collection of Mysterious Myths & Legends

Adrianna had always been fascinated by the mysteries of ancient civilizations. Raised in the rolling hills of England, her childhood was filled with stories of faraway lands and hidden treasures, but none of those tales compared to the allure she had for Egypt... a land of golden deserts, monumental pyramids, and a mythology as interesting, as deep as the Nile River itself. As an archeologist, Adrianna sought the truth behind such myths, but never did she expect to become part of one, one with mere darkness.

The year was 1924, and Adrianna found herself boarding a ship bound for Alexandria. Her auburn hair gleamed in the sunlight, her green eyes alight with great excitement. She was a woman ahead of her time, driven by an insatiable curiosity and an unshakable determination to uncover as many secrets as she could that was long buried beneath the sands of Alexandria. What she would unearth in Egypt, however, was not just mere history, but something far darker, and far more eternal.

Arrival in Egypt

Adrianna's first few weeks in Egypt were consumed with nothing but her work. She joined a team of fellow archeologists who helped her excavate the ruins of Amarna, a city once ruled by the heretic pharaoh Akhenaten. The oppressive heat was relentless, but she reveled in the challenge. The fragments of ancient pottery, faded hieroglyphs, and crumbling statues whispered to her of a time long past, forgotten. The mere sights of the city of Alexandria were breathtaking.

Nestled along the shimmering Mediterranean coast, Alexandria was a city that marries the ancient with the modern, the mythical with the tangible. It was a place where the echoes of history reverberated through bustling streets, where golden sunlight kissed the azure waters, and where every ancient stone and corner tells a story of past empires, philosophers, and many dreamers. Alexandria was captivating, its mere essence portrayed its multifaceted glory, a city that possessed enchanted poets, many traders, conquerors, and wise scholars for many a millennium.

Alexandria stretched like a shimmering jewel along the Mediterranean Sea, its natural harbor protected by the islands of Pharos, which in antiquity bore the lighthouse of Alexandria. The city's geography was defined by its coastal location, with wide promenades, sandy beaches, and the rhythmic cadence of waves against its shores. The Corniche, a grand waterfront boulevard, hugged the curve of the majestic coastline. Flanked by majestic buildings, palm trees, and lively cafes, it is a bustling artery of life where locals and visitors alike could gather to bask in the sea breeze. The salty tang of the ocean mingled with the aroma of grilled seafood from nearby places to eat within the markets, offering a sensory experience that was unique to Alexandria. The Mediterranean itself was a canvas of changing moods. On calm days, its mere surface gleamed like molten sapphire, while on stormy evenings, it roared against the breakwaters, a mere reminder of nature's untamed power. Fishermen dotted the waters in their brightly painted boats, their large nets wide in search of the day's catch, a scene that has remained unchanged for centuries.

To walk through Alexandria was to walk through layers of history. Founded by Alexander the Great in 331 BCE, the city was envisioned as a hub of great culture, commerce, and knowledge. It quickly grew into one of the most significant cities of the ancient world, a place where Greek, Egyptian, and Roman influences blended seamlessly. No description could be complete of Alexandria without mentioning its most iconic institution, the Great Library. Though the library is lost to time, its mere legacy remains a defining feature of the city. Scholars from across the ancient world once gathered here, drawn by its unparalleled collection of many ancient scrolls and manuscripts. The library symbolized humanity's thirst for ancient knowledge, its ambition was to unravel the great mysteries of the cosmos. The mere spirit of the Great Library still lives on in the Bibliotheca Alexandrina, a more modern architectural marvel that stands as both a mere tribute to the ancient library and a mere beacon of contemporary learning, especially for archeologists. Its sleek, sunlit design, an immense disk-like structure tilts towards the sea, reflects the merging of past and present.

Rising majestically above the ruins of ancient temples was Pompey's Pillar, a Roman triumphal column that towers over the city. Carved from red Aswan granite, it stands as a monument to Roman Alexandria, a city that thrived under imperial rule. Nearby lies the remnants of the Serapeum, a grand temple dedicated to Serapis, a deity that symbolized the fusion of Greek and Egyptian religious traditions. Wandering these ruins, one could almost hear the ancient chants of long forgotten priests and the murmurs of worshippers who once filled these sacred places.

Modern Alexandria was a city that brimmed with life. Its streets were a kaleidoscope of colors and sounds, bustling markets rubbing shoulders with elegant homes, and street vendors hawking their wares amidst the hum of passing trams. The souks of Alexandria were a sensory delight. At Souk El-Attarine, the spice market, the air was thick with the earthly aromas of cumin, cinnamon, and cardamom. Vendors displayed mounds of fragrant herbs, their vibrant hues ranging from deep turmeric yellow to fiery paprika red. Buyers would haggle over the prices, their mere voices a symphony of Arabic that added to the market's chaotic charm. Another notable marketplace was the Fish Market near the harbor. Here, the day's freshest catch was on display, gleaming mackerel, swordfish, and prawns piled high. Fishermen's voices rose above the din as they called out prices, their weathered hands quick and deft.

Alexandria's streets reflected its cosmopolitan heritage. French-style patisseries stood next to traditional Egyptian tea houses, while Italian restaurants competed with Levantine baskets. The architectural styles ranged from Ottoman minarets to neoclassical facades, a mere testament to the city's role as a crossroads of different civilizations. Nowhere was this more evident than in the neighborhoods of the city center. Strolling through Raml Station or Mansheya, one could encounter the grand colonial-era buildings adorned with ornate balconies, their faded beauty evoking the city's golden age. The soft pastel hues of these structures contrasted sharply with the vivid advertisements and graffiti that adorned their very walls.

At the western tip of the Corniche stood the Qaitbay Citadel, a fortress built in the early 15th century on the very site of the ancient Lighthouse of Alexandria. Its honey-colored stone walls rose against the backdrop of the vast sea, a bastion of strength that had withstood for centuries of battles and storms. The citadel offered sweeping views of the Mediterranean, its turrets a perfect vantage point to even imagine the mere ships of ancient mariners navigating the very waters.

A haven of tranquility amidst the urban sprawl, Montaza Palace and its sprawling gardens were a favorite retreat for the locals and the tourists alike. The palace, an opulent blend of Ottoman and Florentine architectural styles, sat amidst lush greenery, its red-and-white facade contrasted beautifully with the surrounding palm trees. The lovely gardens were a verdant expanse of manicured lawns, flower beds, and shaded pathways. Families could picnic under the vast trees, couples could stroll hand in hand, and children could chase each other across the green grass. The soft murmur of fountains and the chirping birds lent an air of much serenity.

The relationship between Alexandria and the Mediterranean was intimate and enduring. Beyond the Corniche and the beaches, the city's maritime legacy was evident in its bustling ports and the lives of its seafarers. The Anfoushi neighborhood, near the harbor, was a working-class area where the smell of salt and fish filled the air. Narrow alleys lead to the small cafes where fishermen could gather, their mere faces weathered by years of toil under the bright sun. They shared stories over strong cups of tea, their laughter punctuating the rhythm of the tides. The Mediterranean also defined Alexandria's cuisine. Seafood was a staple, and the restaurants along the Corniche served as dishes that celebrate the bounty of the sea, grilled mullet, spicy calamari, and shrimp prepared with local spices. The mere flavors were vibrant, the portions generous, and the meals often accompanied by the faint music of the waves crashing against the shore.

Alexandria had long been a muse for many writers, poets, and various artists. The city's literary heritage was most famously captured in the old tales, a series of novels that would portray Alexandria as a mere labyrinthine world of intrigue, passion, and great mystery. The city's influence was also evident in many of the painters' works and in the many poets who passed upon these shores, making the city a deep nostalgia that exists as much in memory as in reality. Art galleries and cultural centers thrived in Alexandria, showcasing both traditional Egyptian art and contemporary works. The Mahmoud Said Museum, housed in a beautiful villa, was a treasure trove of modern Egyptian paintings, while smaller galleries in the city center offered glimpses into the vibrant artistic scene. The true heart of Alexandria was its people... warm, hospitable, and very proud of their city's heritage. Alexandrians embodied the mere spirit of their city, a blend of openness and resilience. Life here was lived at a pace dictated by the mere rhythms of the sea and the calls of the muezzin echoing from minarets. Children would play games in the narrow alleyways, their mere laughter ringing through the heated air. Elderly men would often gather at street-side cafes to sip strong, hot teas, Turkish coffees, and play backgammon, their mere conversations punctuated by hearty laughter. Women would linger in traditional abayas shops alongside others in more modern attire, a testament to the city's diverse and evolving culture.

Alexandria's charm lied in its contradictions. It was both ancient and modern, chaotic and serene, a city of many shadows and much light. Whether you stood in the heart of Pompey's Pillar, gazing at the horizon from the Qaitbay Citadel, or simply sipping hot tea at a small cafe overlooking the Corniche, one could not help but be enchanted by the timeless allure of this Mediterranean jewel of a city. To simply explore Alexandria was to embark on a vast journey through a forgotten time, to simply lose oneself in the stories whispered by its streets, and to find much beauty in its every ancient corner.

But, for Adrianna... she longed for the mere 'sands' and the hidden relics beneath them...

One evening, as the sun dipped below the horizon, painting the heated desert in shades of crimson and gold, Adrianna found herself alone at the edge of the dig site. She had been translating a set of inscriptions discovered near a collapsed temple. The symbols hinted at something unusual, references to a forgotten mythical god associated not with sun, like Ra, but with the darker shadows. Her Egyptian guide, a wiry man named Karim, noticed her lingering, "Miss Adrianna," he called, his voice edged with slight unease. "This is not a place for you to dwell after dark."

"Why not?" she asked, her voice, her mere curiosity piqued.

Karim hesitated, glancing at the encroaching shadows. "There are stories... of those who wander here at night. They never return."

Adrianna dismissed his warning with a mere smile, though she couldn't deny the strange chill that crept down her spine. She stayed just a little longer, her fragile, gentle fingers tracing the mysterious glyphs as the desert winds whispered secrets she could not quite understand. That same night, Adrianna searched and read through many old books and ancient documents on the many myths and legends of this place...

Alexandria, the glittering jewel of Egypt's Mediterranean coast, had always been a city shrouded in mystery and lore. From its founding by Alexander the Great to its role as a center of ancient learning, Alexandria had been a mere crossroads of many civilizations. This meeting of different cultures birthed a wealth of several myths and legends, blending Greek, Egyptian, Roman, and later Arab traditions into mystical stories that continued to captivate the imagination. The myths and dark legends of Alexandria told many tales of mythical gods and heroes, of lost treasures and cursed artifacts, of mummies buried beneath the deep sands, of scholars and mystics who had sought to unravel the hidden secrets of the mere universe, the desert itself. These many stories formed a tapestry as rich and intricate as the city itself, weaving together themes of great ambition, knowledge, love, and destinies. The story of Alexandria began with its legendary founder, Alexander the Great. In 331 BCE, as he conquered his way through the ancient world, Alexander dreamed of creating a city that would serve as a beacon of Greek culture and learning. The legend goes that the very location of Alexandria was chosen by a divine will. According to the myth, Alexander the Great consulted the oracle of Zeus-Ammon at Siwa Oasis before actually founding the city. The oracle proclaimed that the mythical gods had ordained a great destiny for him, and that a city built near the Nile's mouth would unite the lands of the East and the West. Inspired by this mere prophecy, Alexander selected the site of modern-day Alexandria, where he reportedly drew the city's outline in flour to seek the blessing of the great gods. Ancient texts and documents describe an omen that occurred during the city's founding. As Alexander marked the city's boundaries, birds swooped down and ate all the flour, which his advisors interpreted as a sign that Alexandria would become a thriving hub of trade and culture, attracting people from all corners of the world. The gods, it seemed, had already deemed Alexandria a city destined for much greatness.

One of the seven wonders of the Ancient World, the Lighthouse of Alexandria (Pharos) was not just an architectural marvel but also a source of countless legends. Built during the reign of PtolemyII Philadelphus in the 3rd century BCE, the lighthouse stood on the island of Pharos, guiding ships safely into Alexandria's bustling harbor. One enduring legend surrounding the lighthouse involves a magical mirror installed at its peak. Ancient sailors believed the mirror had the power to magnify distant objects, allowing guardians of the city to see enemy ships approaching from miles away. Some versions of the mythical tale claimed that the mirror could harness sunlight to set invading ships aflame, protecting Alexandria from naval threats. Though many historians debate the mere existence of such a device, of such a mirror, the myth persists, adding an air of great mystery to the great lighthouse. The lighthouse was also said to be cursed. Some sailors whispered that the Pharos was protected by the spirits of drowned mariners, who would unleash storms upon those who dared to disrespect its sanctity. Stories told of many ships that had vanished near the lighthouse, their crews had been claimed by vengeful spirits. To this day, the mere ruins of the lighthouse, submerged beneath the sea, are still rumored to hold the restless souls of those who perished near its shores.

The Great Library of Alexandria was perhaps the most famous symbol of the city's golden age. As a repository of the ancient world's civilization and collective wisdom, it housed thousands of old scrolls and manuscripts from across the known world. Yet the library's reputation was as a center of mere learning has been rivaled by the myths and legends that had surrounded its fate. One of the most enduring legends tied to old library involved the mythical Book of Thoth. According to Egyptian lore, this sacred text was written by Thoth, the god of wisdom, and contained secrets of the heavens, the earth, and the underworld. It was said that the book granted its reader unparalleled knowledge, including the mere ability to communicate with animals, control the elements, and even glimpse into the future. Some stories claim that a copy of the Book of Thoth was actually hidden within the Great Library, protected by enchantments to prevent unworthy individuals from accessing its power. Others suggested that the book was destroyed in the library's fires, its knowledge forever lost in time, though many whispers still persist that fragments of the text still exist, scattered across the world.

The destruction of the Great Library was itself a subject of myth and speculation, the many fires a whisper through time. While historical accounts vary, legends abound regarding the many causes and mere consequences of the library's demise. Some blame Julius Caesar's siege of Alexandria, while others point to early Christian or Muslim rulers seeking to erase pagan knowledge. One tale suggested that the library's destruction was not merely accidental but merely deliberate, a divine punishment for humanity's hubris in attempting to accumulate all the wisdom and knowledge of the great gods, another story claimed that the library's secrets were not destroyed but simply spirited away by a secret, divine order of wise scholars who had pledged to guard the sacred knowledge until the world was ready to use it wisely.

The Serapeum, dedicated to the mythical god Serapis, was one of Alexandria's most important religious sites. Serapis, a fusion of Greek and Egyptian deities, was worshipped as a mere god of healing, fertility, and the afterlife. The temple became a focal point for many miracles and mythical occurrences. One of the most famous legends of the Serapeum involved its massive statue of Serapis. It was said that the statue could communicate with its worshippers, answering their many prayers with divine signs. Priests claimed that Serapis himself would manifest during the times of great crisis, his voice echoing through the temple to guide his people. When the Serapeum was destroyed in 391CE during the rise of Christianity, some believed the statue's destruction unleashed a curse upon the city. Stories spread of strange, dark omens... earthquakes, storms, and fatal plagues, that followed the temple's fall, interpreted by some as the mere wrath of Serapis for the loss of his sacred space, his sacred temple.

The whereabouts of Alexander the Great's tomb remained one of the greatest unsolved mysteries of Alexandria. According to historical accounts and documentation, Alexander's body was interred in the city that he had founded, in a grand mausoleum befitting his status as one of history's greatest conquerors, but the mere tomb was never definitively located, giving rise to numerous myths. One legend suggested that Alexander the Great's tomb was hidden beneath the streets of modern Alexandria, guarded by an eternal protector. This mere guardian, said to be a colossal stone statue animated by divine magic, would awaken if the tomb was ever disturbed. The myth claimed that the guardian would unleash destruction upon anyone who dares to violate the sanctity of Alexander's final resting place. Another tale posits that Alexander's body was imbued with divine essence, rendering it incorruptible. Some believe that the tomb holds not just his remains but also valuable artifacts of immense power, such as a golden crown that grants immortality. The search for Alexander's tomb has inspired many generations of adventurers and archeologists, all in hopes of uncovering the secret truth behind the mere myth, the mere legend.

Like much of the Arab world, Alexandria had its share of legends involving djinn... a supernatural being made of smokeless fire, often depicted as either benevolent or malevolent spirits. In Alexandria, djinn was said to haunt abandoned buildings, the mere ruins of ancient temples, and the catacombs beneath the city, along with the dry sands of the desert. The Catacombs of Kom El Shoqafa, a vast underground necropolis, were a source of eerie tales. Locals spoke of many shadowy figures and whispered voices that echoed through the labyrinthine corridors. Some even believed that the catacombs were a gateway to the spirit world, where djinn guard the souls of the departed and punish those who trespassed without any respect. Another legend tells of a djinn who resides in Alexandria's harbor, taking the mere form of a glowing orb of bright light that danced across the vast waters, the mere waves of the sea. Sailors claimed that the djinn could grant safe passage or doom their ships, depending on their conduct of character. Offerings of coins or prayers was said to appease this maritime spirit.

The proximity of Alexandria to the Mediterranean had given rise to many tales of sirens, mythical sea creatures who would lure sailors to their doom with enchanting songs. According to local legend, these sirens dwelt near the sunken ruins of the ancient Lighthouse of Alexandria. Fishermen and sailors told of hearing hauntingly beautiful melodies drifting over the water on moonlit nights. Some believed that these sirens are the spirits of those who had perished when the lighthouse collapsed, their very souls trapped in the vast sea forever. The mythical sirens were both feared and revered, seen as a reminder of the sea's brutal beauty and peril.

Another legendary tale, the obelisks known as Cleopatra's Needles, originally erected in ancient Egypt and later transported to London and New York, was steeped in much myth. Legends claimed that the removal of these small monuments from Alexandria angered the gods, bringing misfortune to all those who dared to disturb them. Many stories of unexplained accidents, mysterious deaths, and storms that plagued the ships that transported the obelisks. Some even believed that the obelisks were cursed by Cleopatra's hand and were meant to remain in their original home as eternal symbols, relics of her mere reign and Egypt's glory.

Another tale was of Cleopatra herself... Adrianna had always been drawn to strong, enigmatic women from history. As an archeologist, her mere fascination often led her to uncover stories hidden beneath layers of sand and time, but no historical figure captured her imagination more than Cleopatra VII, the last queen of Egypt, a woman whose name had become synonymous with much power, beauty, and tragedy. When Adrianna arrived in Egypt to begin a new chapter of her career, she also found herself irresistibly drawn to the city of Alexandria, Cleopatra's city. It was here, amidst the faint whispers of the ancient world and the vibrant energy of the present, that Adrianna would uncover a mystery connecting her own life to the legendary queen in ways she could never have imagined. As she continued her research in the quiet of her room, she pondered on the mere discoveries that she uncovered thus far, in her search for the queen's resting place...

Cleopatra VII was not merely a ruler; she was a symbol of resilience in the face of impossible odds. Born in 69 BCE into the Ptolemaic dynasty, she inherited a kingdom rife with political instability. At a young age, she mastered the mere art of diplomacy, spoke multiple languages, and understood the delicate balance of power required to maintain Egypt's sovereignty against the looming shadow of Rome, yet Cleopatra's story was often reduced to her mere romance with Julius Caesar and Mark Antony, overshadowing her intelligence, political acumen, and the cultural renaissance she fostered in Alexandria. She was a woman who defied the mere expectations of her time, wielding power not as a puppet of Rome but as a sovereign determined to preserve Egypt's independence. For, Adrianna, Cleopatra was more than just a historical figure, she was an inspiration, but as Adrianna delved deeper into the queen's life, she began to sense that Cleopatra's story wasn't merely confined to the pages, the mere documents, of history. There was something about Alexandria itself, something alive, that seemed to carry Cleopatra's spirit. When Adrianna first arrived here, she was immediately struck by the city's timeless allure. The bustling streets, the shimmering Mediterranean, and the whispers of all the ancient history that seemed to converge in a symphony that resonated deep within her very soul. Her work brought her to the site of Kom El-Dikka, an archeological treasure trove on her second night in the city, it had once been part of the ancient city's grand center. Among the ruins, Adrianna unearthed artifacts with her team, before going to the desert, that hinted at Cleopatra's reign... fragments of jewelry, shards of pottery bearing inscriptions in Greek and Demotic script, and a series of coins bearing the queen's mere profile. Each small discovery felt like a thread connecting her to Cleopatra, pulling her closer to a truth buried beneath centuries of sand. On this first site, Adrianna sifted through the remains of a collapsed structure, she uncovered a small alabaster box, worn and very tattered. Inside was a small, delicate scroll, its papyrus fragile but surprisingly intact. The glyphs on the scroll seemed to shimmer in the fading light, and as Adrianna read the text, she realized it was a letter, a plea for aid, written in Cleopatra's own hand.

The letter was addressed to an unknown alley, a mere call for support during the tumultuous days leading up to the Battle of Actium. Cleopatra's words were poignant, filled with much determination and sorrow. She had written of her love for Egypt, her fears for her children, and her struggle against the mere forces that sought to subjugate her kingdom, but there was something else... a cryptic line at the end of the ancient letter that sent chills down Adrianna's spine... 'To the one who finds this, know that I entrust you with my story. In Alexandria lies my truth, hidden where the earth meets the stars. Seek it, and you will know me as I truly was.'

The words seemed to speak directly to Adrianna, as if Cleopatra herself had reached across the centuries to leave her a simple message. Determined to uncover the queen's 'truth', Adrianna began a quest that would take her deep into the heart of Alexandria's myths and dark legends. Cleopatra's connection to the goddess Isis was also well-documented. She often depicted herself as the living embodiment of Isis, a powerful symbol of divine authority and motherhood. Adrianna theorized that the queen's 'truth' might be hidden in a temple dedicated to the mythical goddess. Adrianna's research had led her to an obscure reference in ancient texts, a description of a lost sanctuary beneath Alexandria, said to house the very secrets of Isis. With the help of her Egyptian guide, Karim, Adrianna explored the city' labyrinthine catacombs, following a series of glyphs that seemed to point the very way. After a few days, nights, of searching, Adrianna had discovered a hidden chamber beneath Kom El Shoqafa. The air was thick with the scent of earth and age, and the walls were adorned with intricate carvings of Isis, her outstretched wings a mere symbol of protection and power. At the center of the darkened chamber stood a sarcophagus, its worn lid inlaid with pure gold and lapis lazuli. Inside, Adrianna found not a body, or a mummy, but a collection of ancient scrolls and old artifacts. Among them was a diadem bearing Cleopatra's insignia and a beautifully crafted dagger inscribed with a phrase in Greek, 'For those who would defend the light'.

The lovely, gold dagger became the centerpiece of Adrianna's research. It was unlike any artifact that she had encountered, or found, before. Its mere craftsmanship was both exquisite and otherworldly. Legends spoke of Cleopatra's personal dagger, a mere weapon that she had carried as a symbol of her sovereignty and her readiness to fight for her people, but the inscriptions suggested it held more than symbolic value. As Adrianna delved deeper, she discovered references to a ritual associated with the golden dagger, a sacred ceremony meant to invoke the eternal protection of the goddess Isis. According to the ancient texts, the ritual could only be performed by someone who was deemed worthy, pure of heart, someone who understood the mere balance between power and compassion. Adrianna couldn't shake the feeling that the gold dagger was actually calling to her, its purpose unfinished, but she also felt a growing unease, as if she were being watched. The sensation grew stronger as she uncovered more about the sacred ritual, and on this very night, it culminated in a shadowy figure appearing in her mere dreams. In Adrianna's dream, she stood in the Temple of Isis, the golden dagger in her hand. Before her was Cleopatra herself, her presence luminous yet haunting. The queen spoke, her voice like a melody of mere strength and sorrow. "You have come far," Cleopatra said, her dark eyes piercing, "You seek my truth, but are you prepared to bear it? The light you carry is fragile, and the shadows of this world are ever hungry. You must keep searching for my remains under the sands of the desert. I want to be found, just not by anyone. You must have a pure heart, one that has no sins."

Adrianna tried to respond, but her voice caught in her throat. Cleopatra stepped closer, placing a hand over Adrianna's heart... "Do not fear, girl," she said, "You are more like me than you realize. We are bound by our undying love for knowledge, our passion for life, and our defiance of fate, but remember, power without purpose is a flame that consumes."

When Adrianna awoke, her heart racing, the dream felt more real than any she had ever experienced. 'Was it merely her vivid imagination, or had Cleopatra truly spoken to her across the great divide of worlds?'

Within a few days, Adrianna's discoveries soon attracted the attention of many rival archeologists and treasure hunters. News of the golden dagger and the ancient scrolls spread quickly, and Adrianna found herself caught in a web of much intrigue. Competing factions sought to claim Cleopatra's legacy for their own purposes, some for profit, others for prestige, some merely wanted to discover her remains for their own success. Adrianna knew she couldn't allow the ancient artifacts she just discovered fall into the wrong hands. With Karim's help, she worked to secure the underground site, even as she faced many threats, though harmless, and sabotage. The struggle became a slight battle not just for historical preservation but for the integrity of Cleopatra's story, her mere legacy. After intense study, Adrianna finally pieced together the sacred ritual of the gold dagger. It was a simple ceremony meant to honor Isis and channel her eternal protection, a way to safeguard the 'light' that Cleopatra had spoken of in her dream, but the ritual also required a personal sacrifice... a willingness to let go of any fear and embrace one's true purpose. Adrianna performed this sacred ritual in the hidden chamber, her hands nervous, yet steady, as she held the golden dagger aloft. The room seemed to come alive with energy, the mere carvings on the walls glowing softly. As she completed the final invocation, a mere slit of her palm, letting the blood drops fall, a vision unfolded before her... Cleopatra standing at the helm of a ship, her eyes fixed on the horizon, her faint expression was one of unyielding resolve, power. The vision filled Adrianna with a profound sense of connection, as if she had glimpsed not only Cleopatra's strength but her vulnerability. In that moment, Adrianna strangely understood that Cleopatra's 'truth' was not merely about her power or legacy, it was about the courage to face one's own destiny, no matter the price. The vision slowly faded away as Adrianna stood speechless.

Adrianna returned to her work, her mere search for Cleopatra's remains within the ruins of the sands with a renewed sense of purpose. Cleopatra's story had always been one of resilience and defiance, and Adrianna felt such honor to have seen the vision of such a great queen, she felt honored to carry her legacy forward. The artifacts, the golden dagger, the ancient scrolls, were all entrusted to a museum in Alexandria, where they could inspire others to seek the truth behind the many myths and legends of Cleopatra.

But Adrianna's journey here was not over, as she stood on the shores of the Mediterranean that late evening, gazing at the massive waves that had once carried Cleopatra's ships, she felt a quiet certainty that queen's spirit still lingered near her, and in the depths of her heart, Adrianna knew the Cleopatra's story was now part of her own, a bond forged across the ages, a mere testament to the enduring power of such courage, knowledge, and love. So, Adrianna continued her quest to find Cleopatra's remains, and she thought it best to never speak of her vision, her mere encounter in her dream, that she experienced with the legendary, deceased queen...

As Adrianna prepared for her nightcap, she pulled the blanket down and crawled into bed... tomorrow was a new day, a day to discover new artifacts, or if she was lucky, to actually discover Cleopatra's remains, but before she fell asleep, she thought of the last article she had read. A fragile document about an untold myth... a mere legend, it was that of a creature who was supposed to survive on 'blood' alone, who walks the 'sands' of the desert at night, a dark spirit, who preys on the weakest of individuals who may linger just a little too long after dark. Before her eyes closed for the night, she remembered Karim's words at the site earlier... 'Stories... of those who wander the dark, they never return.'

The encounter...

Some nights later, drawn by an explicable pull, Adrianna ventured deeper in her search for Cleopatra's remains, deeper into the ruins, lingering much longer than the rest of the team. The full moon bathed the desert in silver, casting eerie shadows over the broken columns and weathered statues. She carried a lantern, its flickering dim light carving a fragile path through the vast darkness. She stumbled upon a hidden chamber, its entrance concealed by a tangle of sand and stone. With considerable effort, she slowly pried open the heavy, broken door, revealing a staircase that descended into the darkness of the chamber. Adrianna's heart was pounding in her chest as she descended the fragile stairs, her lantern barely illuminating the crypt-like space. At the bottom, she found herself in a grand hall. The walls were adorned with many intricate carvings depicting scenes of worship and blood sacrifices. At the center of the room stood a sarcophagus, its surface inlaid with obsidian and dull gold. An overwhelming sense of dread filled the faint air of the chamber, but Adrianna couldn't turn back now. She knew she was about to find something great, something no one had ever found, she could feel it, yet deep within herself she was hoping it was Cleopatra's remains. She was wrong...

As she approached, the lid of the sarcophagus shifted. A tall, dark figure emerged, radiant and impossibly graceful, with very pale skin, as pale as the moonlight and eyes that glowed crimson red in the lantern's dim light. He was clad in robes of black and pure gold, his presence exuding a power that froze her in place. She wanted to run, to scream, but she could not move. This creature was like a living 'mummy', but she knew it could not be so.

"Who dares disturb my slumber, this night?" the creature asked, his voice deep, a velvet growl.

Adrianna swallowed hard, her voice trembling with much fear, "I... I am Adrianna, an archeologist. I mean you no harm."

The man, the mummy, no, the creature, stepped closer, slowly, his intense gaze piercing through her. "An archeologist," he mused, a faint smirk playing on his lips. "How quaint. Do you know exactly what you have awakened, girl?"

Adrianna could barely breath at this point, but she bravely managed to ask, "Who are you? What are you?"

"I am Kaelen," the creature replied. "Once a prince of this very land, of these very sands. Now, I am a guardian of its many secrets. An immortal fiend, one who dwells alone."

Adrianna suddenly realized that the legends, the myths of the creature who dwells at night within the desert sands, it was all true. She had awakened an immortal demon, a vampire, a mere being of many myths and nightmares, yet, as terrifying as he was, she could not look away from him. His eternal presence was amazing, magnetic, his mere, dark beauty was mesmerizing. Before he could come any closer to her, Adrianna finally gained the courage within her to run away. The creature did not follow after her, but he remained in the chamber only smiling.

Adrianna fled quickly that night, but she couldn't escape the mere thought of Kaelen. He appeared to her in her dreams, his deep voice a seductive whisper that kept calling her back to the desert ruins. By day, she tried to immerse herself in her work, but her thoughts were merely consumed by the mysterious creature, the vampire. Though she couldn't remember exactly where the hidden chamber entrance was, she kept looking in the mere direction as if it would just reappear, but nothing emerged, only sand and wind blew in that direction.

Kaelen, the vampire, was intrigued by Adrianna. Unlike the countless others over the centuries, who had accidentally stumbled over his tomb, his hidden chamber, Adrianna was not as afraid to seek his knowledge, she actually spoke to him with questions before fleeing. Her mere intellect and fiery spirit stirred something within him, a flicker of humanity that he thought he had long ago extinguished.

Their next encounter was not by mere chance. Kaelen appeared at her camp site one late evening just after sundown, after her team had made their departure for the night, his movements silent as a shadow. Adrianna was slightly fearful as she confronted him, her fear tempered by more fascination. "Why do you haunt me so?" she demanded.

Kaelen chuckled, his fangs glinting in the moonlight. "You simply intrigue me, Adrianna. It's as if I have known you before, you remind me of the courageous woman, the queen, that I once knew. You are unlike any of the others that I have encountered."

"Am I supposed to be flattered by that?" she said back in reply, her mere defiance masking her trembling hands.

"You very well should be," he said, stepping closer, "I have lived for many centuries, seen many empires rise and fall, yet you... you are a complete mystery to me, one that even I cannot seem to unravel."

Adrianna hated the way this creature's words made her heart race; the way she felt a slight hint of compassion swelling up within her. She merely hated that she found herself being drawn to him, despite everything she knew about the evil darkness that he represented, the mere lives he had brutally taken over the many years.

As the weeks passed, Adrianna and Kaelen became more frequent in their encounters with each other. Adrianna was too afraid to tell anyone of this creature, yet she longed to see him. Kaelen slowly revealed small fragments of his past... a prince, once a human man, betrayed by his own court, cursed to an eternal existence between life and death, sentenced to be a dark guardian of the desert sands. Adrianna eventually began to share her dreams of uncovering the secrets of Cleopatra, her passion for the past, the artifacts under the vast sands of the desert. Kaelen shared ancient tales that he had ventured through over the centuries, including his knowledge of Cleopatra. Some of their conversations consisted of much tension, agreements and disagreements, making their connection undeniable. Yet, Adrianna struggled with her inner feelings. She knew she couldn't truly love him, he was a cruel creature of nature, of mere evil darkness, a predator to humans for their blood, but her heart betrayed her, yearning for the enigmatic being who had become her closest confidant. Kaelen was torn also. For centuries, he had kept his distance from mortals, seeing them as fleeting and fragile, mere prey, but Adrianna was different, though her blood smelled so inviting. She challenged him, fascinated him, made him feel alive in a way that he hadn't felt in many centuries, manty decades.

One late night, as they stood beneath the starlit sky in the center of the city of Alexandria, Adrianna confronted him, "Why me, Kaelen? Out of all the people in this world, why are you so drawn to me, why are you here with me?"

"Because you simply see me as I am, Adrianna," he said softly, his voice deep. "You see me not as a monster, but as an individual, a man, one who has feelings, one who can actually have the ability to love."

Tears welled in her eyes... "I cannot love you, Kaelen," she whispered, "You are eternal, and I... I am just a fleeting moment in your eternity."

Kaelen cupped her face in his cold hands, his mere touch gentle but forceful, "Perhaps it is the fleeting moments that make my undead life worth living."

Their love, as forbidden, as unorthodox, as it was, grew stronger, deeper, but Adrianna knew this secret love could not last. Kaelen offered her a choice... an eternity by his side, a life beyond the confines of mortality, but the mere price, the cost, was much too great. "I just can't," Adrianna said, her voice saddened, breaking, "I cannot give up who I truly am, what I have worked so hard for. I can't become like you, a mere killer of humans just to survive."

Kaelen's crimson eyes glistened with much sorrow, as a blood tear swelled in the corner of his eye, "Then let me simply protect you, keep you, even if it means that I must let you go."

Adrianna did not respond; she simply kissed his cool lips as tears rolled down her fragile face.

Their final night together was bittersweet. They kissed, caressed beneath the desert moon, the very spot where she had found his hidden chamber, their passion a fleeting blaze against the vastness of all eternity. Adrianna had to return to her world, her heart heavy with the weight of her decision. Kaelen would return to his hidden crypt beneath the sands. With one final kiss farewell, Kaelen said, "I will never forget you, Adrianna. Thank you for these special moments. Now, I must return to my eternal curse as the guardian of these sands. Never forget me."

Years later, Adrianna's many discoveries brought her much acclaim, but her heart remained haunted by the memory of Kaelen. She often found herself gazing at the moonlight, remembering the sands of the desert, wondering if he still watched over her from the shadows like he promised. As she still resided in England, her home, she would always cherish the sweet memories in Alexandria... of the vision of Cleopatra, the many artifacts she discovered, and the love she obtained for the creature of the night, the vampire.

Kaelen, still bound by his curse, remained in the ruins, the sands of the desert in Egypt, still guarding the many secrets of his past, but in the quiet moments of his eternal existence, he allowed himself to remember the one woman, Adrianna, who had brought a ray of light into his eternal darkness.

Though worlds apart, they would always cherish each other's memory, their love would forever endure, a timeless myth, a timeless legend that whispered throughout the sands of the desert winds in Alexandria, a mere testament to the fleeting beauty of a mortal woman's heart and the eternal longing of an immortal man's soul. Their small, brief romance would forever be a collection of the mysterious myths and legends in Alexandria.

The End.

A Collection of Mysterious Myths & Legends

By: Jo Ann Atcheson Gray

A Collection of Mysterious Myths & Legends

www.ingramcontent.com/pod-product-compliance
Lightning Source LLC
Chambersburg PA
CBHW070546180726

47999CB00021B/2314